YOU LOST ME
Discussion Guide

**Starting Conversations Between Generations . . .
On Faith, Doubt, Sex, Science, Culture, and Church**

David Kinnaman
and Aly Hawkins

BakerBooks

a division of Baker Publishing Group
Grand Rapids, Michigan

Published by Baker Books
a division of Baker Publishing Group
P.O. Box 6287, Grand Rapids, MI 49516-6287
www.bakerbooks.com

Printed in the United States of America

Library of Congress Cataloging-in-Publication Data is on file at the Library of Congress, Washington, DC.

ISBN 978-0-8010-1499-4 (pbk.)

The internet addresses, email addresses, and phone numbers in this book are accurate at the time of publication. They are provided as a resource. Baker Publishing Group does not endorse them or vouch for their content or permanence.

The author is represented by Fedd & Company.

12   13   14   15   16   17   18   7   6   5   4   3   2   1

In keeping with biblical principles of creation stewardship, Baker Publishing Group advocates the responsible use of our natural resources. As a member of the Green Press Initiative, our company uses recycled paper when possible. The text paper of this book is composed in part of post-consumer waste.

green press INITIATIVE

SPECIAL THANKS

Heartfelt thanks to Rebecca, Christopher, Derik, Laura, Andrzej, and Ross for sharing your stories with generous honesty. The views they express are their own and do not represent the opinions or positions of David Kinnaman, Barna Group, or Baker Books.

CONTENTS

AN INTRODUCTION TO
YOU LOST ME

View "An Introduction" on the DVD

Discuss the Following with Your Group

In addition to David Kinnaman, six people are featured in this video series. They are

- Rebecca, an actor
- Andrzej, a welder
- Christopher, a seminary student
- Laura, a fashion entrepreneur
- Ross, a scientist
- Derik, a comic book artist

Which person or people do you most identify with from their comments in the introductory clip? Why?

David Kinnaman introduces three types of "you lost me" stories. *Nomads* identify as Christians but are not active in the church or in their pursuit of Christ. *Prodigals* have left both the church and Christianity—they no longer identify as Christians. *Exiles* are passionate about faith in Christ but feel torn between church expectations and engagement with the wider culture.

If you are a young adult, which of these stories do you most identify with? Why?

If you are an older adult, which of these stories have you observed playing out among young adults in your family and/or faith community? How?

David views Barna Group's research, such as the scientific surveys and interviews done for *You Lost Me*, as a bridge that can help different groups of people better understand each other. What do you hope to accomplish as your group begins this study?

Spend some time in group prayer as you bring this session to a close or before moving on to "Session 1: Overprotective." Pray for the Spirit to grant wisdom and guide your community's conversations during the next few weeks.

Session 1

OVERPROTECTIVE

Before your group session, take the following self-diagnostic to prepare for conversation.

1. Anything that is not Christian is evil or sinful.

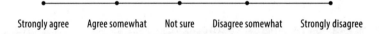

Strongly agree   Agree somewhat   Not sure   Disagree somewhat   Strongly disagree

2. It's a good idea to make strict rules about what I watch, read, or view online.

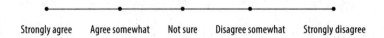

Strongly agree   Agree somewhat   Not sure   Disagree somewhat   Strongly disagree

3. The Bible has a straightforward answer for every issue.

Strongly agree   Agree somewhat   Not sure   Disagree somewhat   Strongly disagree

4. Life is one big gray area.

Strongly agree   Agree somewhat   Not sure   Disagree somewhat   Strongly disagree

5. Nothing I watch, read, or view online can harm me.

Strongly agree   Agree somewhat   Not sure   Disagree somewhat   Strongly disagree

6. The best way to serve God is by working in a church or other Christian endeavor.

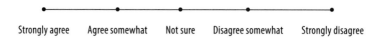

Strongly agree   Agree somewhat   Not sure   Disagree somewhat   Strongly disagree

7. The Bible is complicated and sometimes hard to understand.

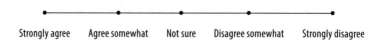

Strongly agree   Agree somewhat   Not sure   Disagree somewhat   Strongly disagree

8. God wants to redeem human culture, not destroy it.

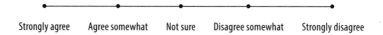

Strongly agree   Agree somewhat   Not sure   Disagree somewhat   Strongly disagree

9. Being "in but not of the world" means separating ourselves from non-Christian influence.

Strongly agree   Agree somewhat   Not sure   Disagree somewhat   Strongly disagree

10. I want to use my gifts and skills to participate in and influence culture.

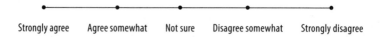

Strongly agree   Agree somewhat   Not sure   Disagree somewhat   Strongly disagree

Notes

_____

_____

_____

_____

_____

_____

_____

_____

_____

_____

_____

_____

_____

_____

_____

_____

_____

_____

_____

_____

_____

Let the Conversation Begin

View "Session 1: Overprotective" on the DVD

Discuss the Following with Your Group

In the video, David observes that the church sometimes minimizes transcendent or meaningful experiences that occur outside the church, whether they happen in nature, at a museum or concert, or elsewhere. Has your experience of the church been similar or different? In what way?

Christopher, a seminary student, is the young Asian man featured in the video. He says visiting an art museum on a Sunday morning, rather than going to a church service, puts him "in dialogue with God." Where do you best experience God's presence? Why?

Laura, the British fashion entrepreneur, suggests that Christians often overemphasize the divide between sacred and secular. Do you agree or disagree with her assessment? Why?

David echoes Augustine and Aquinas's belief that all truth is God's truth. How might the church do a better job celebrating truth wherever it is found?

According to *You Lost Me*, many young people have been discouraged through their Christian upbringing from exposure to secular films, TV, music, and other media. The adults who have warned them away from these influences believe that anything not overtly Christian has the potential to mislead or corrupt impressionable young minds. Based on your answers to the Five-Minute Prep, do you think Christians should protect and separate themselves from secular culture? Why or why not?

In contrast, many teens and twentysomethings—and some older adults too—view their cultural surroundings in a positive light. Secular films, TV shows, music, and so on are often meaningful and enriching, and many young adults value the opportunity to participate in culture by creating, not just consuming, content such as music and video. In what ways do you think Christians should engage with and participate in secular culture?

In *You Lost Me*, David suggests that there are inherent risks associated with following Christ. What types of risks might be diametrically opposed to our fear- and security-oriented culture?

In the video, Derik, the bearded comic book artist, talks about his struggle to read and interpret the Bible with the Christian community. He feels that getting caught up with questions about whether various Bible stories should be understood literally misses the point. What are some risks you see in setting aside questions like these?

With every risk comes a possible reward. If your faith community were to take a risk and make space in the conversation about Scripture for people like Derik, what are some rewards or positive outcomes that could result?

Laura says that, in the past, fashion became an idol in her life, but continuing her work in the industry is worth the risk because it is what God created her to do—it is her calling. Do you agree or disagree that the risk is worth it? Why?

Laura goes on to say that she is also passionate about inspiring
people to live fully into their calling, the unique vocation to which
God has called them. As you think about your calling, even if you're
not completely clear about what it is, what are the risks you must
take to answer God's call?

Is it worth the risk? How can you know?

*Spend some time in group prayer as you bring this session to a close.
Set aside time for those who want prayer specifically for discernment
as they seek to follow God's call. Then pray for the Spirit to guide
the ongoing conversation about risk-taking and discernment in your
faith community.*

Keep Talking (and Listening)

The following questions will help you and your group keep the conversation going. If you can, make time in the coming week to connect with one or two of your group members to continue the discussion.

In what ways is our church (or ministry or other group) overprotective of children, teens, and young adults? What is the motive behind our overprotectiveness? Is God calling us to change? How?

How is our church (or ministry or other group) teaching discernment? What needs to change in order for us to train more effectively?

How can parents and ministry leaders work together to shape our children's hearts to be responsive and obedient to God, regardless of the risks?

Session 2

SHALLOW

Before your group session, take the following self-diagnostic to prepare for conversation.

1. Church is more about teaching the Bible than cultivating relationships with others.

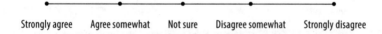

Strongly agree   Agree somewhat   Not sure   Disagree somewhat   Strongly disagree

2. It's important to be deeply connected to people in my church.

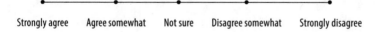

Strongly agree   Agree somewhat   Not sure   Disagree somewhat   Strongly disagree

3. We have a youth/college pastor whose job is to mentor our young people.

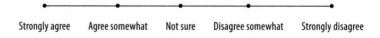

Strongly agree   Agree somewhat   Not sure   Disagree somewhat   Strongly disagree

4. I have a strong friendship with one or two church people from a different generation.

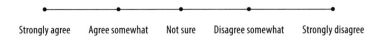

Strongly agree   Agree somewhat   Not sure   Disagree somewhat   Strongly disagree

5. We expect young adults to be involved in leading our church.

Strongly agree   Agree somewhat   Not sure   Disagree somewhat   Strongly disagree

6. Young people should listen and learn.

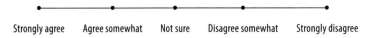

Strongly agree   Agree somewhat   Not sure   Disagree somewhat   Strongly disagree

7. I connect with church friends on Sunday and that's enough.

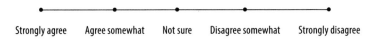

Strongly agree   Agree somewhat   Not sure   Disagree somewhat   Strongly disagree

8. The size of our youth/college group shows that young people are growing in Christ.

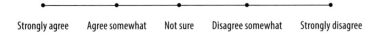

Strongly agree   Agree somewhat   Not sure   Disagree somewhat   Strongly disagree

9. My relationships at church help me to think critically about my life and choices.

Strongly agree   Agree somewhat   Not sure   Disagree somewhat   Strongly disagree

10. I experience the presence of God when I worship with my whole faith community.

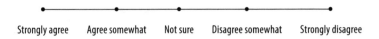

Strongly agree   Agree somewhat   Not sure   Disagree somewhat   Strongly disagree

Notes

Let the Conversation Begin

View "Session 2: Shallow" on the DVD

Discuss the Following with Your Group

In the video, David uses the image of a car to explain the way many young adults experience Christianity. Driving off the lot with all the confidence in the world, they soon find it doesn't hold up as promised—the bumpers fall off and the windshield turns out to be cellophane instead of glass. Like that car, Christianity doesn't seem equal to the challenges of the road. Is your experience of faith similar or different? In what way?

Christopher, the seminary student, likens church to a Band-Aid, a cover for the wounds of churchgoers, rather than a place where wounds can be uncovered and truly healed. Why do you think so many churches struggle to be communities where people can be completely honest without fear of being judged?

David suggests that the shallowness of young people's experience of church has to do partly with a lack of depth in the church and partly with a willingness on the part of young adults to remain shallow. Do you agree or disagree with his assessment? Why?

Which of these—shallow church or willfully shallow young Christians—do you think is most at work in your faith community? Why?

.

David points out in the video and in *You Lost Me* that many churches separate the different generations for activities and sometimes worship so that these experiences can be tailored to fit the preferences of the audience. Based on your answers to the Five-Minute Prep, how important are intergenerational relationships in the life of your church?

David contends that apprenticing young people, one-on-one, into following Christ is more effective than big events. Do you agree or disagree? Why?

What effect could a mentor/apprentice relationship have on Christopher's experience of church? How might his perceptions about church change?

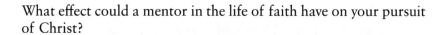

What effect could a mentor in the life of faith have on your pursuit of Christ?

What effect could apprenticing someone in the life of faith have on your pursuit of Christ?

David tells the story of a woman in her seventies who is upset by what she perceives as a lack of respect from the younger generation— they don't know her name. She doesn't seem to think it's a problem that she doesn't know *their* names, however. How do you think this mindset contributes to making the church, in Christopher's words, "a source of injury"?

Christopher expresses discomfort with the influence of media and entertainment on churches, which turns churchgoers into passive consumers. Instead of sitting back and receiving, he says, we should be giving something of ourselves to each other. What might this look like for you?

What would you have to sacrifice in order to apprentice a younger sister or brother in the faith? What would you have to sacrifice in order to be mentored by an older sister or brother in the faith?

Spend some time in group prayer as you bring this session to a close. Pray specifically for the Spirit to guide the ongoing conversation about apprenticeship and intergenerational relationships in your faith community.

Keep Talking (and Listening)

The following questions will help you and your group keep the conversation going. If you can, make time in the coming week to connect with one or two of your group members to continue the discussion.

In what ways do the older adults in our church (or ministry or other group) apprentice children, teens, and young adults to be Christ-followers? In what ways do younger Christians mentor older adults? How can we support these relationships and expand connections between generations?

In what ways are young people an integral part of our church's or ministry's life? What are some additional ways they can contribute to our overall health? How can we ensure that they are becoming servants of the church, not just consumers of the church's services?

How are we communicating our expectations for the important role young people have in the life of our church or ministry? How can we provide meaningful rituals and rites of passage that demonstrate both our committed care and our high expectations?

Session 3

ANTISCIENCE

Before your group session, take the following self-diagnostic to prepare for conversation.

1. There can be harmony between matters of science and matters of faith.

Strongly agree   Agree somewhat   Not sure   Disagree somewhat   Strongly disagree

2. The claims of science threaten Christianity.

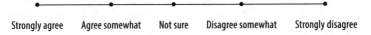

Strongly agree   Agree somewhat   Not sure   Disagree somewhat   Strongly disagree

3. It is impossible to believe the Bible and believe in evolution.

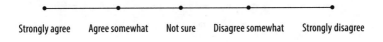

Strongly agree   Agree somewhat   Not sure   Disagree somewhat   Strongly disagree

4. When scientific evidence contradicts a faith claim, we should reevaluate our beliefs.

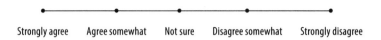

Strongly agree   Agree somewhat   Not sure   Disagree somewhat   Strongly disagree

5. Science cannot answer the most important questions about our existence.

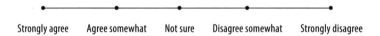

Strongly agree   Agree somewhat   Not sure   Disagree somewhat   Strongly disagree

6. Studying science often leads to a loss of faith.

Strongly agree   Agree somewhat   Not sure   Disagree somewhat   Strongly disagree

7. The disease-fighting possibilities of stem cell research are worth the price.

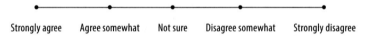

Strongly agree   Agree somewhat   Not sure   Disagree somewhat   Strongly disagree

8. Science's impact on the world has been more positive than negative.

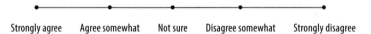

Strongly agree   Agree somewhat   Not sure   Disagree somewhat   Strongly disagree

9. Part of the Bible's purpose is to communicate accurate information about the natural world.

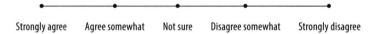

Strongly agree   Agree somewhat   Not sure   Disagree somewhat   Strongly disagree

10. Scientists are unbiased and impartial, with no agendas of their own.

Strongly agree   Agree somewhat   Not sure   Disagree somewhat   Strongly disagree

Notes

Let the Conversation Begin

View "Session 3: Antiscience" on the DVD

Discuss the Following with Your Group

Ross, the young scientist in the video, suggests that the relationship between the church and science has historically been characterized by the scientific community's desire to ask questions and the church's desire to limit questions. Has your experience been similar or different?

Ross says the need for God as the explanation for unanswered questions has decreased as scientific knowledge has increased. He suggests that, instead of relegating God to the shrinking realm of unexplained phenomena, Christians should shift their understanding of God to align with scientific discoveries about our existence. Do you agree or disagree? Why?

How would your view of God change if you were to take his advice?

Based on your answers to the Five-Minute Prep, do you think it is possible for young people to trust both scientific knowledge and the wisdom of historic Christianity? Why or why not?

David says in the video that part of the problem for many Christians and faith communities is the sheer volume of scientific information: it's impossible for everyday people of faith to become experts on every issue raised by science! He suggests that believers in scientific careers are a vital resource for churches wrestling with these issues. How could these Christians help the broader faith community?

David contends that the church must find a way to speak prophetically to our culture about issues of "making life, faking life, and taking life."* *Making* life includes issues such as fertility science, human cloning, and stem cell research; *faking* life includes technologies such as digital implants and artificial intelligence; and *taking* life includes questions of end-of-life care and weapons of warfare, among others. How can the church speak credibly to the wider culture on issues such as these?

* Thanks to Nigel Cameron, director of the Center on Nanotechnology and Society, research professor of bioethics, and associate dean of the Chicago-Kent College of Law in the Illinois Institute of Technology, for this helpful formulation.

The list below is not comprehensive, but each topic relates in some way to making, faking, or taking life.

Your group leader will choose one or two of the following topics to discuss as a group. Try to share your point of view humbly and to listen lovingly to those with a different view.

- *Information technology.* The way we consume information has drastically changed in the past twenty years, and hyper-connectivity—the ability to access anything, anytime, from anywhere—is changing the way humans interact and even, some studies suggest, how we think. What are the possible positives and negatives, spiritual or otherwise, that might arise as a result? What can the church do to help?

- *Human health.* Medical advances are just the tip of the iceberg when it comes to human health. How will the church respond to questions about ethical food consumption, the obesity epidemic, genetic research and therapies, fertility and reproduction, and the proliferation of chemicals in consumer goods (just to name a few)? What can the church offer to a culture that is increasingly interested in holistic human flourishing?

- *The natural world.* This includes questions about climate change, conservation and exploitation of natural resources, exploration of space, physics and the study of matter, and our relationship to animals and other species—as well as questions about how we and our universe came into existence. How can the church respond with wisdom to discoveries of science?

Ross says he has often been frustrated in his attempts to talk with Christians about science's understanding of the natural world because they do not rely on evidence but on claims of faith. How could Christians become better conversation partners with science-minded believers and nonbelievers?

The conflict between science and faith is partly due to friction between two distinct ways of knowing: science relies on human *reason* while faith relies on divine *revelation*. How could acknowledging these two valid sources of knowledge lead to more fruitful dialogue?

Ross suggests that what science reveals about the natural world is awe-inspiring. In what ways might mutual wonderment at and contemplation of creation build a bridge between believers and nonbelievers?

Spend some time in group prayer as you bring this session to a close. Pray specifically for the Spirit to guide the ongoing conversation about science and faith in your faith community.

Keep Talking (and Listening)

The following questions will help you and your group keep the conversation going. If you can, make time in the coming week to connect with one or two of your group members to continue the discussion.

How does our church (or ministry or other group) fuel the fire of conflict between science and faith? Conversely, what are we doing to make peace and sow wisdom? In what ways are we helping or hindering our desire to pass on a vibrant faith to young people and equip them to live faithfully in a science-dominated culture?

What are some ways we can create opportunities in our community for dialogue about making life, faking life, and taking life? Who is equipped to guide these discussions? How can we ensure that people of differing views are welcome and respected?

How do we nurture the gifts and interests of children, teens, and young adults who are drawn to careers in science? How could we improve in this area?

Session 4

REPRESSIVE

Five-Minute Prep

Before your group session, take the following self-diagnostic to prepare for conversation.

1. The topic of sex should not come up in Christian conversation.

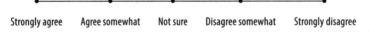

Strongly agree   Agree somewhat   Not sure   Disagree somewhat   Strongly disagree

2. Sexual satisfaction is an important part of personal fulfillment.

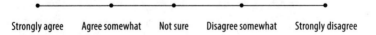

Strongly agree   Agree somewhat   Not sure   Disagree somewhat   Strongly disagree

3. Waiting for sex until after marriage is unrealistic and even unhealthy.

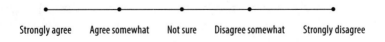

Strongly agree   Agree somewhat   Not sure   Disagree somewhat   Strongly disagree

4. The Bible's teaching about sex and sexuality is clear and unambiguous.

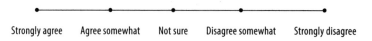

Strongly agree   Agree somewhat   Not sure   Disagree somewhat   Strongly disagree

5. My choices about sex are nobody's business but mine.

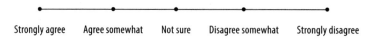

Strongly agree   Agree somewhat   Not sure   Disagree somewhat   Strongly disagree

6. As long as no one gets hurt, sexual activities like "friends with benefits," sexting, viewing porn, and hooking up are good ways to let off steam.

Strongly agree   Agree somewhat   Not sure   Disagree somewhat   Strongly disagree

7. Procreation is the main purpose of sex.

Strongly agree   Agree somewhat   Not sure   Disagree somewhat   Strongly disagree

8. There is something shameful about sexual pleasure.

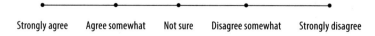

Strongly agree   Agree somewhat   Not sure   Disagree somewhat   Strongly disagree

9. Getting married and having a family are two options among many related to my sexual choices.

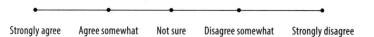

Strongly agree   Agree somewhat   Not sure   Disagree somewhat   Strongly disagree

10. Watching movies or TV shows that depict sexual situations is not appropriate for Christians.

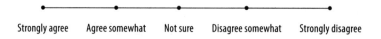

Strongly agree   Agree somewhat   Not sure   Disagree somewhat   Strongly disagree

Notes

Let the Conversation Begin

View "Session 4: Repressive" on the DVD

Discuss the Following with Your Group

David suggests in the video that sex is a challenge for most, if not all, humans, because sexuality and sexual activity involve the whole person: body, mind, heart, and soul. As you think about Rebecca, the young woman featured in the video, which of these seems to challenge her most? What makes you think so?

What, if anything, about Rebecca's story resonates with you? What, if anything, about her story makes you uncomfortable?

You Lost Me makes the case that there are two competing narratives about sex at work in the lives of Christian young adults. The *traditionalist* view wants to keep sex out of sight, to sweep it under the rug. There is something dirty about sex and sexual pleasure, even within marriage, so the "Christian" thing to do is refrain from talking about it. The *individualist* view, in contrast, wants to make sex the centerpiece of personal fulfillment. The highest goals of sex are not just pleasure but freedom and self-expression, and that means commitment, chastity, fidelity, and family are options to exercise if and when they are "right for me." Based on your answers to the Five-Minute Prep, with which of these competing narratives about sex do you agree more? Why?

Which of these narratives is most portrayed by Rebecca's story? Why do you think so?

How do you think the traditionalist view could be harmful? What about the individualist view?

In *You Lost Me*, David suggests that neither traditionalism nor individualism is the biblical ethic of sex. Instead, "we need to rediscover the *relational* narrative of sexuality" (p. 160). In the video, he suggests that one way we might begin to recapture this relational ethic is by sharing honestly with one another about sexual issues.

Your group leader will choose one or two of the following topics to discuss as a group. Try to share your point of view humbly and to listen lovingly to those with a different view.

- **Marriage.** The Bible uses marriage as a powerful metaphor for the self-sacrificing love God has for humanity, demonstrated ultimately on the cross of Christ. In contrast, much of our marriage talk today, both inside and outside the church, is me-centered. How can we rediscover the profoundly sacred and sacrificial nature of both marriage and sex? How can we reclaim marriage as a communal, not just personal, covenant?

- **Gender.** In the relational narrative of sexuality, women are given full and complete responsibility to be their God-given best. They are neither walking wombs (traditionalism) nor walking vaginas (individualism). How can we mentor young women to become confident Christ-followers who are honored and respected in the church? How can we encourage young men to become strong, compassionate servants of God, their family, and their friends?

- **Sexual orientation.** Christian or not, younger adults tend to be more accepting of gay, lesbian, bisexual, and transgender individuals than older adults. How can we engage in meaningful dialogue, reflecting our relational priority even when we disagree with others? How can we welcome all people to be a part of God's family while adhering to the church's historic interpretation of Scripture regarding homosexuality? (See pp. 163–64 of *You Lost Me.*)

In the video Rebecca says that, in her experience, church is not usually a place where people receive healing for their sexual hurts because sex is not often talked about in honest, personal terms. How has your experience with church been similar or different?

David suggests that reclaiming the biblical, relational ethic of sex means sharing with one another our mistakes, pain, and regrets—as well as our healing and joy—regarding our own sexual histories. Do you agree or disagree? Why?

The next few questions are designed to help you begin to share your story. The answers can be discussed as a group or, if you prefer, the larger group can split into pairs. If your group chooses this option, make an effort to partner with someone of a different generation from you.

When you think about your sexual history, do you have pain or regrets? Have you made any mistakes? Share one story.

Do you have a story of healing or joy? Share one.

In the video, Rebecca says she wants to be known for "brave grace." What would "brave grace" look like in your life when it comes to sex and sexuality?

As a group, spend some time in prayer as you bring this session to a close. Set aside time for those who want prayer specifically to heal their sexual past or present. Then pray for the Spirit to guide the ongoing conversation about sex in your faith community.

Keep Talking (and Listening)

The following questions will help you and your group keep the conversation going. If you can, make time in the coming week to connect with one or two of your group members to continue the discussion.

How is our church (or ministry or other group) living the relational ethic of sex? What needs to change in order for us to embody it more fully?

How does God want to use our sexual pasts for his purposes in the present and future? How might "brave grace" characterize our lives and our community?

Are our expectations for the next generation realistic? If we expect young adults to wait for sex until marriage and wait for marriage until their late twenties or early thirties, how are we helping them live abundantly and joyfully until then?

Session 5

EXCLUSIVE

Before your group session, take the following self-diagnostic to prepare for conversation.

1. Other people's beliefs are as valid as mine.

Strongly agree   Agree somewhat   Not sure   Disagree somewhat   Strongly disagree

2. Christians should not date or marry non-Christians.

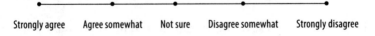

Strongly agree   Agree somewhat   Not sure   Disagree somewhat   Strongly disagree

3. The Bible is clear about who is "in" and who is "out," so the church should be too.

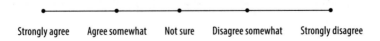

Strongly agree   Agree somewhat   Not sure   Disagree somewhat   Strongly disagree

4. Christians should look a certain way.

Strongly agree   Agree somewhat   Not sure   Disagree somewhat   Strongly disagree

5. Christians should not judge the beliefs or actions of others.

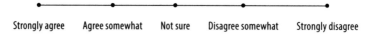

Strongly agree   Agree somewhat   Not sure   Disagree somewhat   Strongly disagree

6. Faith should not get in the way of friendships.

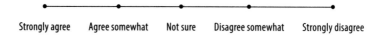

Strongly agree   Agree somewhat   Not sure   Disagree somewhat   Strongly disagree

7. God's Spirit is at work only in the church.

Strongly agree   Agree somewhat   Not sure   Disagree somewhat   Strongly disagree

8. Listening to different religious points of view puts Christian faith at risk.

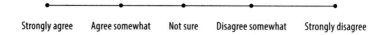

Strongly agree   Agree somewhat   Not sure   Disagree somewhat   Strongly disagree

9. Being fair is more important than being right.

Strongly agree   Agree somewhat   Not sure   Disagree somewhat   Strongly disagree

10. It is better to stay silent than to offend someone by speaking out.

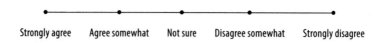

Strongly agree   Agree somewhat   Not sure   Disagree somewhat   Strongly disagree

Notes

Let the Conversation Begin

View "Session 5: Exclusive" on the DVD

Discuss the Following with Your Group

Andrzej, the welder featured at the beginning of the video, recalls feeling as a kid as though he didn't belong in church because of his appearance. Why are there usually expectations for how people should look, act, and talk when they come to church?

What happens when someone doesn't meet the expectations?

Christopher, the seminary student, says that when he returned to church after having wandered for several years, he sat in the back and slipped out early because he feared being met with hostility and judgment by regular churchgoers. Why might some people feel threatened by the church environment?

David suggests that excluding those who are different hurts both those who are excluded and those who do the excluding. Why is that the case?

George Barna coined the term *Mosaics* because young adults in North America are the most diverse generation in terms of ethnicity, religion, socioeconomics, and other markers. They are also globalized in their perspectives like no generation before. How do you think this diversity will shape the church as Mosaics mature and move into leadership?

In the video and in *You Lost Me*, David claims the Mosaic generation is characterized by a strong impulse to include others—and this desire sometimes causes alienation from the church, which is often less inclusive than they would like. Based on your answers to the Five-Minute Prep, how should Christians relate to people with different beliefs, moral standards, or ways of life? Why?

Ross, the young scientist featured in the video, says that from his point of view as a church outsider, Christians who are racist or homophobic do more harm to the church than to anyone else. Do you think this is true? Why or why not?

What could other Christians do to counteract the negative impact of aggressively exclusive believers?

David argues that, in Scripture, God's judgment often reconciles and restores relationships rather than separates or alienates humans from God or from each other. Why do you think Christians sometimes exercise judgment that alienates instead of reconciles?

Laura, the British fashion entrepreneur, says Christians should prioritize relationships; differences in beliefs or ways of living should not become relational barriers between Christians and others. Do you agree or disagree? Why?

What are the risks you see in prioritizing relationships as Laura suggests? What are the possible rewards?

David suggests that Mosaic Christians have the potential to be the next great missionary generation because of their love and compassion for outsiders. What could the church do to equip and support their missionary impulse?

Spend some time in group prayer as you bring this session to a close. Pray for the Spirit to guide the ongoing conversation about your faith community's relationship to outsiders.

Keep Talking (and Listening)

The following questions will help you and your group keep the conversation going. If you can, make time in the coming week to connect with one or two of your group members to continue the discussion.

In what ways does our church (or ministry or other group) embrace those who don't belong? In what ways do we, intentionally or unintentionally, exclude those who don't fit in? What could we do to be more hospitable and compassionate?

How do we handle theological or behavioral disagreements in our community? How can we move toward reconciliation more often than toward alienation?

How are we equipping and supporting the missionary drive of younger generations? How can they help our community as we seek to obey the Great Commandment and the Great Commission?

Session 6

DOUBTLESS

Before your group session, take the following self-diagnostic to prepare for conversation.

1. Doubting is an opportunity to grow closer to God.

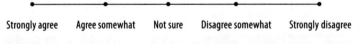

Strongly agree   Agree somewhat   Not sure   Disagree somewhat   Strongly disagree

2. Having doubts is a symptom of weak faith.

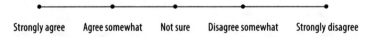

Strongly agree   Agree somewhat   Not sure   Disagree somewhat   Strongly disagree

3. The church is a place where people can ask their most pressing questions without fear of being judged.

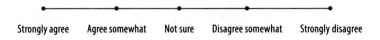

Strongly agree   Agree somewhat   Not sure   Disagree somewhat   Strongly disagree

4. The best response to someone's doubts is to supply an answer for every question.

Strongly agree   Agree somewhat   Not sure   Disagree somewhat   Strongly disagree

5. Strong Christians don't experience depression.

Strongly agree   Agree somewhat   Not sure   Disagree somewhat   Strongly disagree

6. Our community is a safe place for those who doubt their faith.

Strongly agree   Agree somewhat   Not sure   Disagree somewhat   Strongly disagree

7. If someone doubts the basic tenets of Christianity, he or she is not a Christian.

Strongly agree   Agree somewhat   Not sure   Disagree somewhat   Strongly disagree

8. God often uses doubts to deepen faith.

Strongly agree   Agree somewhat   Not sure   Disagree somewhat   Strongly disagree

9. It's okay to disagree with pastors and other leaders on matters of faith or theology.

Strongly agree   Agree somewhat   Not sure   Disagree somewhat   Strongly disagree

10. Pastors and leaders should never express doubt.

Strongly agree   Agree somewhat   Not sure   Disagree somewhat   Strongly disagree

Notes

Let the Conversation Begin

View "Session 6: Doubtless" on the DVD

Discuss the Following with Your Group

Derik, the bearded comic book artist in the video, says that his church growing up was not a safe place to express doubts about the pastor's teaching. "Conform or die" is how he puts it. Has your experience of church been similar or different? In what ways?

David says there seems to be an expectation in many churches that people should leave their doubts at the door. Why do you think this expectation is so common?

Laura, the British fashion entrepreneur, says her experience growing up in church included elements of condescension for her age and gender—because she was a young girl, "we don't need to take you seriously." Is it important to take young people's questions seriously? Why or why not?

David says there is a tendency among Christians to answer legitimate questions with clichés or slogans such as "Let go and let God" or "Hate the sin, love the sinner." Why might phrases like these seem so unsatisfying to those with heartfelt questions?

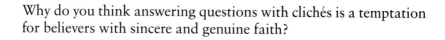

Why do you think answering questions with clichés is a temptation for believers with sincere and genuine faith?

Christians have varying degrees of comfort with doubt. Based on your answers to the Five-Minute Prep, what role, if any, does doubt play in the life of faith?

David suggests that sometimes people struggling with doubt don't take the risk of asking their questions. Which do you think puts faith more at risk: unexpressed doubts or unsatisfying answers to one's questions? Why?

Christopher, the seminary student, says that for him, art is a way of exploring doubt and questions in a more nuanced way than he usually finds in discussion at church. What are some other ways, besides discussion, that believers can explore their doubts in search of deeper faith?

Derik says he has become increasingly comfortable with the phrase "I don't know" when it comes to questions about theology and the life of faith. What is one question you have about God or the life of faith for which your answer is currently "I don't know"?

How could "I don't know" be a good starting point for finding a satisfying answer?

In *You Lost Me*, David suggests that *doing* is a powerful antidote to profound doubt: *doing* actions of faith, such as serving others, participating in corporate worship, studying Scripture with a faith community, and praying, to name a few. Do you think doing can lead us through troubling questions to deeper faith on the other side? Why or why not?

Spend some time in group prayer as you bring this session to a close. Set aside time for those who want prayer specifically for their struggle with doubt. Then pray for the Spirit to guide the ongoing conversation about how to make space for questions in your faith community and how to support those on a quest for answers.

YOU LOST ME Discussion Guide

Keep Talking (and Listening)

The following questions will help you and your group keep the conversation going. If you can, make time in the coming week to connect with one or two of your group members to continue the discussion.

In what ways does our church (or ministry or other group) encourage people to ask hard questions about God and the life of faith? What could we do better?

How do we answer difficult questions? For instance, are we too ready with clichés and slogans? Are we comfortable with "I don't know"? Are we willing to journey alongside those with doubts and questions as they discover answers for themselves? How?

What opportunities do we offer those who doubt to "do" the actions of faith? How can we help them transform deeds into deeper faith?

WHAT'S NEXT?

Let the Conversation Begin

View "Bonus Session: What's Next?" on the DVD

Discuss the Following with Your Group

In the video, each of the six people featured in this series express their hopes for the future, whether for themselves or for the church.

- Andrzej, the welder, hopes that people can overcome their bad experiences with church and other institutions to discover a real, rich relationship with the Savior.
- Christopher, the seminary student, envisions a church engaged restoratively in society, helping to preserve and protect God's creation and to promote justice for those who are oppressed.
- Laura, the fashion entrepreneur, dreams of a church so alive in God's Spirit that Christians become life-giving and redemptive as they seek to fulfill God's calling on their lives, whatever that may be.
- Derik, the comic book artist, hopes to find a balance between stability and freedom as he endeavors to *do* good rather than *get* things.
- Rebecca, the actor, wants God's love in her to bless and enrich the lives of those around her.
- Ross, the scientist, looks forward to an increasingly bright future as people seek knowledge and take action based on truth.

Which person's hopes resonate most with you? Why?

David suggests that Christians may have some apologizing to do to teens and young adults who have found the church to be overprotective, shallow, antiscience, repressive, exclusive, or doubtless. With which of these areas does your community struggle most? Why?

How will you seek to restore the connections between your community and those who have been lost because of that struggle?

Which of the six areas is a strong point for your community, an area in which you are doing well? In what way?

How will you seek to strengthen your community's response to these six areas of disconnection?

David suggests that we are sometimes more attached to the ways we have shaped the church than we are to a desire for young people to help shape the church in ways that are meaningful to them. How much should teens and young adults be involved in visioning the future of your faith community?

You Lost Me and this video series do *not* recommend shaping church around youth or young adults to the exclusion of older generations; rather, David is a strong proponent of intergenerational communities of faith. How could your faith community build relationships between generations as you seek to reconnect with young adults?

What next steps will you take with your community to encourage the faith journeys of the next generation?

Spend some time in group prayer as you bring this series to a close. Pray for the Spirit to guide and strengthen you and your group as you seek to reestablish connections between generations.

LEADER'S NOTES

The *You Lost Me* video series presents key material from the book *You Lost Me* by David Kinnaman, designed to encourage intergenerational conversation among pastors and youth leaders; young adults, teens, and their parents; and adult laypeople of all ages concerned for the future of the church. Ideally, the group you bring together for dialogue will be made up of people from several generations so that group members can listen to and learn from each other as they express their particular points of view.

The *You Lost Me* video series can be presented as a six-, seven-, or eight-week group study.

- If you choose six sessions, view "An Introduction" to *You Lost Me* and "Session 1: Overprotective" during the first group meeting. Use some, all, or none of the discussion questions for "An Introduction to *You Lost Me*," according to your preference, and then move on to Session 1. If you choose to include "Bonus Session: What's Next?" it may be viewed after "Session 6: Doubtless" at the final group meeting.
- If you choose seven sessions, view "An Introduction" to *You Lost Me* and "Session 1: Overprotective" during the first group meeting. Use some, all, or none of the discussion questions for "An Introduction to *You Lost Me*," according to your preference, and then move on to Session 1. Use "Bonus Session: What's Next?" for the final week.

- If you choose eight sessions, view "An Introduction" to *You Lost Me* during the first group meeting. Use the discussion questions to introduce the study material and prepare your group for the coming sessions. Use "Bonus Session: What's Next?" for the final week.

Because rich, honest conversation is the goal, group size is important. We recommend a minimum of six people to ensure different generations are represented, and a maximum of twelve to ensure every person has an opportunity to be heard. If you present the series to a larger group, consider breaking into smaller cells for discussion once everyone has viewed the video session. Each smaller cell should have a point person to facilitate good conversation and should be a cross-section of generations as much as is possible.

Every person should have his or her own *Discussion Guide*. Each of the six main sessions includes a self-diagnostic called "Five-Minute Prep" to be completed before the session begins. If you notice after "Session 1: Overprotective" that some group members were unable to complete the Five-Minute Prep before the session, consider setting aside five minutes at the beginning of the meeting so everyone can be prepared for discussion.

To facilitate meaningful conversation, be aware of who talks a lot and who doesn't (every group has some of both!). Gently invite those who are more hesitant to share their views. You may, on occasion, need to remind the group to give everyone a chance to speak. If conversation becomes heated, as it may when the topic is a hot-button issue, allow people to express themselves passionately (even if it makes others uncomfortable) as long as they are respectful and do not verbally attack anyone else.

Also be aware of time. If your group has agreed to meet for ninety minutes, bring the session to a close at that time. If it seems as though productive dialogue can continue after the agreed-upon time, take a short break at the ninety-minute mark to allow those who need to leave to make an exit without awkwardness or embarrassment.

Special Note for Sessions 3 and 4

"Session 3: Antiscience" and "Session 4: Repressive" offer groups a chance to dialogue about particularly tough issues related to faith-science conflicts (Session 3) and sexuality (Session 4). No group could cover every suggested topic in a reasonable time, so select one or two topics that will resonate most with the members of your group. Make your selections in advance from the suggested topics (see pp. 37 and 47). Plan on an extra dose of sensitivity during these sessions, as well, since many Christians find it difficult to talk about science and sex.

EVERY STORY MATTERS.

HEAR THEM NOW IN THEIR OWN WORDS WITH THE *YOU LOST ME* DVD

HELP A NEW GENERATION FIND FAITH.

Share the groundbreaking ideas in *You Lost Me* with your small group, leadership team, or entire church, with the engaging and interactive new *You Lost Me* DVD, the companion to the Discussion Guide. In fact, this unique resource is designed to help start meaningful conversations between generations.

Filled with candid real-life interviews of young people and insightful observations from author and researcher David Kinnaman, this new tool will inform, equip, and empower groups and churches to understand the unique challenges that are affecting younger Christians.

It's not enough for us to know about the trends. With this video study and discussion guide, you and your group will think deeply about your influence with teens and young adults and discover practical ways to help this generation find faith again.

Examine. Illuminate. Transform.

Relevant. Intelligent. Engaging.

Available anywhere books are sold.
www.youlostmebook.com

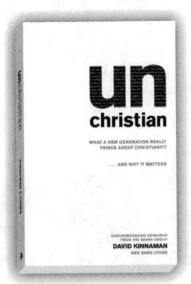